★ IT'S MY STATE! ★
Ohio

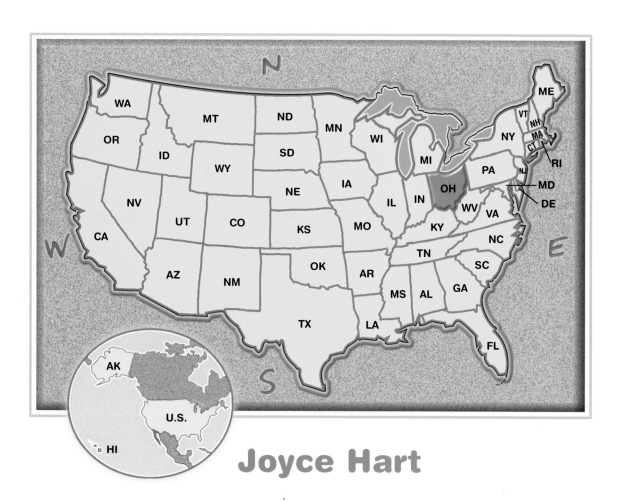

Joyce Hart

 **Marshall Cavendish**
Benchmark
New York

Marshall Cavendish Benchmark
99 White Plains Road
Tarrytown, New York 10591-9001
www.marshallcavendish.us

Photo research by Candlepants Incorporated

Library of Congress Cataloging-in-Publication Data

Hart, Joyce, 1954-
Ohio / by Joyce Hart.
p. cm. -- (It's my state!)
Summary: "Surveys the history, geography, economy, and people of
Ohio"--Provided by publisher.
Includes index.
ISBN 0-7614-1907-1
1. Ohio--Juvenile literature. I. Title. II. Series.

F491.3.H37 2006
977.1--dc22

2005018055

Cover photograph: Layne Kennedy / Corbis
Back cover illustration: The license plate shows Ohio's postal abbreviation followed by its year of statehood.

The photographs in this book are used by permission and through the courtesy of: *Corbis: 11, 36, 37; Bettmann, 24, 38, 41 (bottom),
48 (top), 48 (bottom), 49 (top), 49 (middle), 49 (bottom); David Muench, 9; W. Cody, 12; Hal Horowitz, 17; Mark Bolton, 21 (middle);
Archivo Iconografico, S.A., 34; Charles E. Rotkin, 39; Reuters, 48 (middle); Charles O'Rear, 58; Bruce Burkhardt, 64; Chuck Savage,
71 (top). Index Stock: Jeff Greenburg, 42, 44; Dennis Macdonald, 55. The Image Works: Jeff Greenburg, 47, 51, 56, 73, 74; Jim West, 53,
69; Hinata Haga, 57. Minden Pictures: Tom Vezo, 4 (middle); Mark Raycroft, 4 (bottom); Michael Quinton, 19, 23 ; Jim Brandenburg,
20. SuperStock: 13, 62; Gene Ahrens, 8; Tony Linck, 26; age footstock, 40. Northwind Picture Archives: 27, 28, 29, 33, 41 (top). Animals
Animals / Earth Scenes: Richard Shiell, 4 (top), 21 (top), 21 (bottom); Michael Habicht, 5 (top); McDonald Wildlife Photography, 5
(middle); Breck P. Kent, 20 (bottom). Envision: Mark Ferri, 5 (bottom); Steven Needham, 68; Rita Maas, 70 (top); George Mattei, 70
(middle), 71 (bottom). Peter Arnold, Inc.: Galen Rowell, 10; Jim Wark, 14; Matt Meadows, 16, 70 (bottom); Alex S. MacLean, 66; Ray
Pfortner, 67; Friedrich Stark, 71 (middle); Peter Frischmuth, 72.*

Series design by Anahid Hamparian

Printed in Malaysia
1   3   5   6   4   2

Contents

A Quick Look at Ohio

Nickname: Buckeye State
Population: 11,459,011 (2004 estimate)
Statehood: March 1, 1803

Tree: **Ohio Buckeye**

The name of the buckeye tree comes from a group of Native Americans who believed that the nut of the state tree looked like the eye of a buck (a male deer.) Although the buckeye tree can grow to be 60 feet tall, the average buckeyes in Ohio only reach about half that height. The largest known buckeye tree in the state is located near North Bend in Hamilton County.

Bird: **Cardinal**

In 1933, the red cardinal was chosen as the state bird. The cardinal is known for its very bright color. Male cardinals' feathers are usually red, while the females' tend to be brown. A cardinal also has a distinctive head crest, which is a tuft of feathers on the top of its head.

Animal: **White-tailed Deer**

White-tailed deer live mostly in wooded areas around farmlands. Some of their favorite foods include corn, crab apples, and honeysuckle leaves. In 1988 it was officially named the state animal.

Insect: Ladybird Beetle

The ladybird beetle is the official name of the ladybug, a small red beetle with black spots on its back. Gardeners like ladybugs because they can eat up to 5,000 insects in a lifetime, ridding the garden of many pests. In 1975, when the ladybug was made Ohio's state insect, state legislators stated that this insect was like Ohioans, who are proud and friendly.

Reptile: Black Racer

The black racer helps farmers because it eats rats and other rodents that like to nibble on the farmers' crops. One of the reasons it is such a successful hunter is because it is fast. Some black racers have been recorded going as fast as 10 miles per hour. But beware, the black racer is also very aggressive and can produce a painful bite.

Drink: Tomato Juice

Tomato juice was chosen as the state drink because Ohio is the number one producer of this red, juicy drink. Because the state drink, the state flower, the state insect, and the state bird are all red, there is a group of elementary school students in Ohio working to have red become the official state color.

1 The Buckeye State

From rolling hills, to flat plains, and sandy beachfronts, Ohio is a combination of landscapes. The eastern border of the state starts as rolling plateaus—raised land—and slowly settles into flat plains toward the west. The state's northern border is made up of a long beachfront, which runs along Lake Erie. At the other end of the state, the majestic Ohio River cuts a curving trail from east to west across Ohio's southern boundary.

The Ice Age

The last Ice Age occurred about 10,000 years ago. In an ice age, temperatures drop below freezing and stay there for very many years. During the last Ice Age, most of the land that includes present-day northern Ohio was buried under a huge glacier. This is a thick ice mass that moves very slowly. When a glacier moves, it scrapes against the earth and can flatten hills, fill in valleys, and redirect the flow of rivers. The glacial

Ohio's Borders
North: Lake Erie and Michigan
South: Kentucky and West Virginia
East: Pennsylvania
West: Indiana

7

The Lorain West Breakwater Lighthouse sits on part of Ohio's Lake Erie shore. Lake Erie's natural changes over the years have helped to shape Ohio's geography.

movement in Ohio changed the landscape in many ways. The section now known as the Lake Plain area, or the Great Black Swamp, which is founds in northwestern Ohio, was once a large lake. The Till Plains, located in western Ohio, received its name from the rock debris that covers the land. The rock debris was carried there by the melting glaciers. As the glaciers melted, Lake Erie overflowed. The overflowing water eventually created a small stream, which grew in size and became what is known today as the Ohio River.

The Appalachian Plateau

Most of the eastern half of Ohio is made up of the Appalachian Plateau. This is the most rugged part of the state. Here you will find some of the steepest hills and the deepest valleys in Ohio. The soil in this part of the state is not very fertile, so this is not a farming area. Although forests once covered most of the state, many of them have been cut down. But some of the largest remaining forests, such as Wayne National Forest, still exist on the Appalachian Plateau.

The Appalachian Plateau is also where much of Ohio's richest mineral deposits are located. Coal, for instance, was first found in Jefferson County, on Ohio's eastern border. Since that discovery, Ohio has become one of the biggest producers of coal in the United States. Natural gas and oil are also found there.

A waterfall near Old Man's Cave in Hocking Hills State Park. Ohio's Appalachian Plateau is home to Ohio's Wayne National Forest and several state parks.

In this photograph, the sun rises over a marshy area along the Cuyahoga River in northeastern Ohio.

Marietta is located on the southern part of the Appalachian Plateau. East Liverpool, which is famous for its pottery, is also located on the Appalachian Plateau. Athens, Hocking, and Perry are some of the main coal-producing counties in this area. Akron sits at the northern edge of the Plateau. Akron, with its population of 217,074, is Ohio's fifth-largest city.

The Bluegrass Region

When someone hears the term "Bluegrass Region," they usually think of Kentucky. But this region flows into Ohio, too. The Bluegrass Region, sometimes referred to as the Lexington Plain, is the smallest land region in Ohio and is located in the southern

A horse grazes in a pasture on a small farm in the Bluegrass region. The soil in this region is not very fertile, so most farms located there do not grow large crops.

part of the state. It is made up of rolling hills that are covered in thin but fertile soil. Adams Lake is a beautiful recreation area that is found in the Bluegrass Region. The Shawnee State Forest, one of the largest forests in the state, is also found here. There are no large cities in this area.

The Till Plains

The Till Plains make up most of western Ohio. Although the main feature of this region is low, rolling hills, both the highest and the lowest point in Ohio are located here. Campbell Hill, in Logan County, rises 1,550 feet into the sky, making it Ohio's highest point. At the southwestern corner, along the Ohio River near Cincinnati, is Ohio's lowest point. This point is only 433 feet above sea level. The hills of these plains are made up

Dayton, Ohio's sixth-largest city, is located on the shore of the Miami River.

The city of Cincinnati was founded alongside the Ohio River.

of soil and rocks that were pushed together by retreating glaciers as they melted at the end of the last Ice Age. Most of this area was completely covered in woodlands before settlers moved here and discovered the fertile soil.

The Till Plains has the most fertile soil in Ohio. This is where most of Ohio's farms are located. Farmers grow wheat, corn, soybeans, and cattle there. The fertile soil may have attracted many of the original Ohioans to this area, but in modern times it is the large cities that draw new people to the state. Cincinnati, the third-largest city in Ohio, lies to the south on the Till Plains. Dayton, the sixth-largest city, is just a short drive north of Cincinnati. Columbus, Ohio's largest city, is the state capital and is located in the center of the Till Plains.

The Great Lakes Plains

The Great Lakes Plains covers the entire northern portion of Ohio. This land is also fertile, and many different kinds of fruits and vegetables are grown here. Most of the Great Lakes Plains in Ohio follows the shoreline of Lake Erie. In the northeastern corner, the plains are only 5 to 10 miles wide. The plains widen, however, in the northwestern corner, where they measure more than 50 miles wide.

The city of Cleveland dominates this area with its busy manufacturing, shipping, trading, and recreational areas. Cleveland is Ohio's second-largest city. Other cities in this area, such as Toledo and Lorain, also have ports on Lake Erie, which allows them to ship the products they make to other states or to countries around the world.

An aerial photographs shows Put-in-Bay Island, which is located in Lake Erie.

The Waterways

Many thousands of years ago, Ohio was covered with water. Today much of that water has been drained into more than 60,000 lakes, reservoirs, and ponds and 44,000 miles of rivers and streams. All the rivers and streams in the northern quarter of the state drain into Lake Erie. The other rivers drain into the Ohio River to the south. The major rivers in the state include the Ohio, Scioto, Miami, Sandusky, Huron, and Cuyahoga Rivers.

Lake Erie, part of Ohio's northern border, is Ohio's largest lake and the second smallest of the Great Lakes. But it is not that small. It is the twelfth-largest fresh water lake in the world and is more than 200 miles long and about 57 miles wide. In ancient times, Lake Erie was much deeper than it is today. If you walk along the coastal plain in northwestern Ohio, you might notice beach ridges, which are sandy deposits that rise above the otherwise flat ground. These ridges mark the ancient shoreline and show how high the waters in the lake used to be. Today Lake Erie's deepest point measures only about 200 feet.

Ohioans enjoy other lakes too. Some of the major lakes in Ohio are Berlin Lake, Seneca Lake, C.J. Brown Reservoir, and Grand Lake St. Marys.

The Climate

Ohio's lack of high elevation means that the weather across the state is generally the same for all parts of the state. But this lack of mountainous land barriers also means that if a strong weather system is blowing down from Canada or up from the Gulf of Mexico, there is nothing that will stop that strong weather from entering the state. So sometimes, Ohioans experience very cold and sometimes very hot and stormy weather. Another determining factor is Lake Erie, which can make northern Ohioans a bit colder in the spring. In the fall, people who live along the lake can also expect the temperatures to be a

The lowest recorded temperature was minus 39 degrees Fahrenheit, which occurred in 1899 in Milligan, near New Lexington. The highest temperature was 113 degrees, in 1934 in Gallipolis.

little bit warmer than the rest of their fellow Ohioans.

In January, Ohioans can expect the temperature to linger around 28 degrees Fahrenheit, which is just a little below freezing and perfect for snow. In July, warm, humid weather hangs over the state with an average temperature of 73 degrees. Of course, temperatures vary, with many summer days recording hotter weather some years and colder temperatures in other years. But for the most part, Ohioans spend rather typical winter days snuggled in warm jackets and gloves from about November until March. They enjoy warmer and stormier days, with thunderstorms and sometimes tornadoes possible in the spring and summer. In the fall, the days are crisp and cool.

Residents of certain parts of Ohio are used to snow and ice in the wintertime.

The wettest part of the state is located around Wilmington in the southwest. Toledo and Sandusky, in the northern part of the state, receive the least amount of rain and snow. People who live in northeastern Ohio see the most snow—almost 100 inches each year!

Wildlife

Ohio has many wild plants. A wide range of flowers and trees grow in Ohio's forests, plains, and fields. Plants of special interest to many Ohioans are the wild plants they can eat. On the list of edible plants are nuts, such as those found on the shagbark hickory tree. This hickory tree is also the source for a delicious syrup. Native Americans used to make a refreshing drink for the berries of the red sumac shrub. A plant that produces a fruit similar to a banana actually grows in the river valleys of Ohio. The fruit is called a pawpaw fruit and is long and green in color

Pawpaw trees—and their tasty fruit—grow in different parts of many eastern states, but pawpaw trees can be found in every region of Ohio. Some towns even hold festivals honoring this fruit.

when it is ripe. Many people enjoy eating pawpaws, but wild animals find the pawpaws in the fall as soon as they are ripe.

Mushrooms also grow in different parts of the state. In the spring, morel mushrooms pop out of the ground. When prepared properly, this mushroom can be very tasty. However, an expert needs to be the one to pick the mushrooms because many mushrooms can be poisonous when eaten. So when you pick wild plants to eat, any of them from nuts to berries, make sure you or someone with you can properly identify them.

The state is also home to a variety of animals. Different types of birds fly through the Ohio skies and nest in its fields and trees. Fish, amphibians, and other aquatic animals live in Ohio's lakes, rivers, and streams. In the forests are woodland creatures such as raccoons, opossums, squirrel, bats, rabbits, and deer. Ohio has populations of snakes, turtles, salamanders, and frogs, too. Larger animals, like wolves, cougars, bison, and elk, used to live in Ohio, but these animals require very large wilderness areas, which Ohio no longer has.

The black bear is an example of an animal that used to roam throughout the whole state at one time. But by 1850, there were no black bears left in Ohio. The forests were being cut down, and the bears had no place to live. But black bear populations are coming back because many of the forests are expanding. Scientists recently counted more than 100 bears in Ohio, and some of them were females with cubs. This means that the black bear population continues to grow.

Black bears are not the only animals with growing populations in Ohio. Some types of eagles are also returning. In 1979 there were only four nesting pairs. Today, there are more than fifty pairs. Eagles were endangered at one point, partly due

Over the last ten years, black bear sightings have increased in Ohio. This is because the bear populations have increased in Ohio and its surrounding states.

to a loss of habitat, but also because of the use of pesticides. Pesticides, chemicals that kill insects, eventually wash into the rivers and lakes and contaminate fish. Eagles eat the fish and are poisoned by the pesticides. Now many of those pesticides are banned, so the fish and the eagles are growing healthier.

There is a similar story about the beaver, which once was very numerous in Ohio. Trappers received a lot of money for beaver skins at one time. By 1830, there were no beavers left. Beaver skins were not as popular in the mid-1900s, so trappers lost interest in them. That was when the beaver population in the state began to improve. In the 1970s, it was estimated that more than 5,000 beaver lived in Ohio. Scientists today believe that the beaver population has increased to more than 25,000.

Plants & Animals

Cicada

Although many Ohioans call this insect a locust, it is really a cicada. The mating call of the cicada is produced by the male, who vibrates his drum-like abdomen in order to attract females. The sound of the cicada has become so much a part of Ohio summers, it would not seem like summer without it.

Weasel

Weasels can be found in almost all of the states but their numbers are especially high in Ohio. There are so many weasels in Ohio that they are still hunted for their fur. Weasels live in forests as well as on Ohio farmlands, as long as there is some water nearby. They are known for their ability as mousers. Catching and eating mice is one of the weasel's specialties.

Perch

The yellow perch is native to Ohio's waters and can be found in lakes, ponds, and slow moving rivers. This fish, which is golden yellow with black stripes, prefers clear water with sandy bottoms.

Persimmon Tree

The persimmon tree is a native tree in Ohio, and grows in the southern part of the state. The persimmon produces a delicious fruit that ripens in the fall and is often included in many Thanksgiving celebrations. It was a common food of Native Americans, who dried the fruit and ate it throughout the winter. The wood of the persimmon tree is very hard and is sold to businesses that make wood heads for golf clubs and cue sticks that are used in shooting pool.

Trillium

The trillium is Ohio's state wildflower. Its name comes from the Latin word for "three" because it has three large ruffled petals and three large oval leaves. Trillium flowers are found in every part of Ohio in the early spring. Because a trillium blooms about the same time that robins migrate back to Ohio, the flower used to be called a "wake robin."

Scarlet Carnation

Dr. Levi L. Lamborn was reportedly the first person to grow carnations in the United States. Dr. Lamborn gave his first carnation to William McKinley—an Ohioan who would later become the president of the United States— to wear in the buttonhole of his jacket. After that, McKinley was often seen wearing carnations. Because of this, in 1904, the scarlet carnation became Ohio's state flower. Many carnations are grown in Alliance, which is called Carnation City.

Endangered Animals in Ohio

There are many reasons why animals become endangered, and for the peregrine falcon, the cause is insecticides. These poisons are sprayed on crops, which the falcon eats, and then causes the eggs of the falcon to form improperly. Because of this, fewer falcons are born each year. The peregrine is one of the fastest birds in North America. It can fly 60 miles per hour. But when it dives to catch its dinner, the falcon can go as fast as 200 miles per hour.

The trumpeter swan is also endangered in Ohio. The trumpeter swan is all white with a black beak. It is the largest swan that exists. The last time a wild trumpeter swan was seen in the state was 1900. Recently, however, the state developed a plan to raise trumpeter swans in zoos, then release several pairs each year so that by 2006 there will be at least 150 swans living in the wild.

With its beautiful and distinctive four-season climate, its wood lands and city landscapes, its long beaches both on lakes as well as along riversides, Ohio offers a wide variety of things to see, to explore, and to experience. It is no wonder wild animals are returning to this state. They, like the people who live here, like making Ohio their home.

Baby trumpeter swans—called cygnet—stay close to their mother. Because of their low populations in the wild, Trumpeter swans are an endangered species in Ohio.

2 From the Beginning

The Ancient People

After studying tools left behind by ancient peoples who once lived in caves in the Ohio Valley, scientists and historians have estimated that people lived in the area of Ohio for many thousands of years. One discovery suggests that some of the first people lived here as far back as 13,000 BCE. Most of these early people hunted wild animals and gathered wild fruits and nuts. They followed wild herds of animals and did not build permanent structures to live in. These early groups are called the Paleo-Indians and the Archaic People.

About 3,000 years ago, another group of ancient people appeared. The most well known of these ancient people are referred to as the Adena. These people began to grow crops such as squash and sunflowers. Because they needed to tend their gardens, they built permanent places in which to live. They also constructed mounds in which they buried their dead and items they treasured. The most famous Adena mound is the Great Serpent Mound found in Adams County.

The 1930s were a hard time for the country. These Ohioans marched to the capitol in Columbus to demand help from the state government.

An aerial photograph shows the Serpent Mound in Adams County. This amazing mound is nearly a quarter of a mile long and has been designated a National Historic Landmark.

Another group, called the Hopewell people, lived in Ohio around the same time as the Adena. They built huge mounds similar to those of the Adena. The Hopewell were also known as great traders. They traded with Native groups from as far away as the Atlantic Coast, the Gulf Coast, and the northern shores of Lake Superior. Both the Adena and the Hopewell people seem to have disappeared from the Ohio area, but no one knows why.

The Great Serpent Mound is 1,330 feet long, and at one end, you can see the serpent's open jaws. Inside the serpent's mouth is an oval shape, which some people believe represents an egg.

There is not much known about the people who came to this area after the Hopewell and Adena. However, there is evidence that a group of people, whom scientists have called the

Fort Ancient people, lived in the southern Ohio area. These people might have been related to Native people from Mexico. In the northern area, a group named the Whittlesey Focus people lived as farmers. Both of these groups disappeared, however, and by the middle of the seventeenth century, all groups of Native Americans in the Ohio area were gone.

The names *Ohio* and *Buckeye* both come from Native American languages. *Ohio* is an Iroquois word for "something great or beautiful." *Buckeye* is a translation of the Native word *hetuck,* which means "the eye of a buck." Some Native Americans referred to the tall, white early settlers as *hetuck,* suggesting that the settlers reminded the Native Americans of the tall buckeye trees.

The Historic Peoples

One theory concerning the departure of early Native American peoples from Ohio is that the powerful Iroquois, from the area of present-day New York, killed all remaining Natives in the Ohio area. The Iroquois were in search of new hunting grounds, and they found Ohio rich in wildlife and

Many of the Native American groups who settled in the region that now includes Ohio came from other parts of the country.

edible plants. The constant Iroquois attacks made other people afraid to live in the Ohio area, so the land was uninhabited for almost sixty years.

Around the middle of the eighteenth century, French traders created settlements in the Ohio area, and the power of the Iroquois began to decline. Because the Iroquois were no longer a threat, small groups of Native Americans began to move into the Ohio area once again. One tribe, called the Huron, moved from Canada and settled around the Sandusky River Valley.

The Miami people came from the west. They set up villages along the rivers that now bear their name: The Great Miami and the Little Miami. Even some bands of Natives from the Iroquois Nation moved to Ohio around this time. In Ohio, the Iroquois were known as the Mingoes. The Mingoes settled mostly in eastern and central Ohio. The Delaware people lived in eastern Ohio. And the Shawnee, who were pushed out of Pennsylvania by European settlers, lived in southern Ohio.

Many of these groups were used to living close to Europeans by this time. The Europeans wanted furs, which the Native Americans supplied. In return, the Native hunters received metal axes, knives, and other

At first, European traders depended upon Native Americans to provide them with beaver pelts and other animal skins.

tools. Sometimes the Europeans paid for the furs with fancy colored beads. Sometimes they sold the Native Americans guns, ammunition, and alcohol. Unfortunately, some traders paid the Native people with alcohol. Many Native Americans began to forget about the ways that their parents and grand-parents had taught them to live off the land.

French and English Control

Throughout most of the seventeenth and eighteenth centuries, France and England fought over the right to claim the land that was referred to as the Ohio Country. This parcel of land included most of what would become Ohio as well as portions of Indiana, West Virginia, and Pennsylvania. Both France and England had set up fur-trading companies in these territories and they fought fiercely with one another for the animal skins that Native Americans brought in. Both the French and the English people tried to convince the Native people to join them in their wars. However, in 1763, a final clash between the French and English occurred in what is called the French and

Indian War. England won the war and the right to claim all of the Ohio Country. This did not, however, end the fighting.

After the Revolutionary War, many colonists moved from the eastern states into the Ohio Territory in search of more land and new homes.

The Game of Quoits

The game of horseshoes developed from the ancient game of quoits. This game was played in Ancient Greece more than 2,000 years ago, and eventually became popular throughout English colonists brought the game to North America, where it later became the game of horseshoes.

What You Need

Rope or clothesline-60 inches (5 feet)
Ruler
Scissors
Yarn – 12 inches each of two different colors
Packing tape or duct tape
Round wooden stake - at least 1 foot long (you can use a branch or a stick or a wooden dowel)

Cut the rope into four 15-inch pieces. Cut the yarn into four 6-inch pieces.

Wrap one piece of yarn around one piece of rope. Use the other three pieces of yarn on the other three pieces of rope.

Loop each piece of rope into a circle with the ends touching. Use the tape to keep the ends together. Add as much tape as you need to keep the rope in a ring shape. You should have four rings of rope-two in one color and two in the other.

Push the stake into the ground. About 15 feet away, mark a tossing line. You can use a piece of string or a branch to mark the tossing line.

How to Play

Each player team has two quoits (rope rings) of the same color. Each player takes a turn tossing both quoits toward the stake. After the first player throws his or her two rings, the other player throws his or her rings.

If your quoit encircles the stake—called the hob— you get 3 points. The quoit closest to the hob scores 1 point. If one player's quoit lands on top of the other player's quoit, no points are earned.

Take turns tossing the quoits until someone reaches 21 points. That person is the winner!

Although the English did not have to worry about the French any more, they did have troubles with the Native people. Native Americans were not very happy about more white settlers moving onto their land. To prevent more hostilities, the English set up boundaries to help separate the white people from the Native people. White settlers were not allowed to claim any land west of the Appalachian Mountains. Unfortunately for the Native people, the United States government had other plans. The Revolutionary War was about to be fought, and when the United States defeated the English in 1776, white settlers were encouraged to move into Ohio.

The Northwest Territory

In 1784, Thomas Jefferson laid out boundaries of a tract of land that referred to as the Northwest Territory. The land's borders were: to the west, the Mississippi River; to the south, the Ohio River; and to the north, the Great Lakes. Three years later, the Northwest Ordinance was established. This document set up how the land was to be divided and governed.

According to the Northwest Ordinance, The United States Congress selected the first person who would act as governor. As soon as five thousand male landowners lived in the territory, they could elect their own legislature, which included a house of representatives and a legislative council. Later, when sixty thousand people lived in one portion of the territory, they could apply for statehood.

In, 1788, Arthur St. Clair became the first governor of the Northwest Territory. And Marietta, Ohio, was declared the first capital of the Territory. On March 1, 1803, there were enough people living in the eastern portion of the

Northwest Territory for Ohio to apply and become the first state carved out of the Territory and the seventeenth state of the United States of America.

The End of Tecumseh's Dream

Although Ohio was now an official state, this did not mean that the problems between the white settlers and the Native Americans were solved. By the 1800s, many Native groups in Ohio were suffering. In their attempts to supply the Europeans with furs, Native Americans had over-hunted the land. With the animal populations dwindling, the Native people had trouble finding food.

Native leaders became concerned about their people and the loss of their land. The Shawnee chief, Tecumseh, and his brother, who was called the Prophet, tried to bring all the remaining Native groups together. They thought that if the tribes united, they would be strong enough to stop the white settlers from taking over their land. United States General William Henry Harrison knew of Tecumseh's plans and attacked and destroyed

Prophetstown, the largest Shawnee village. Tecumseh was not there at the time, so he survived. However, two years later, in 1813, Tecumseh and his men joined forces with the British Army in Canada in an

Through the early 1800s, Native Americans continued to clash with Americans who wanted to settle the land in Ohio.

attempt to defeat General Harrison's soldiers in another battle. The United States Army had twice as many men as the British and the Native American forces, and the Army won. Not only were the Native Americans defeated, but Tecumseh was killed in this battle. After Tecumseh's death, there was no more talk of uniting to fight the white settlers.

The New State

After Ohio was declared a state, white settlers were encouraged by the government to move into the area. By the middle of the 1800s, more than two million people populated the state. Prior to the 1800s, most people living in the Ohio area were farmers who grew crops like corn, beans, and melons. After Ohio became a

The Ohio River was important for trade and travel in many Ohio cities. This painting shows Cincinnati in the 1800s.

state, agriculture became a major business. Farmers planted apple and peach orchards and shipped the fruit to the East Coast. Tobacco was also planted and processed into smoking materials. To process these crops, many factories were built. Other factories were built to produce farm equipment like tractors and reapers.

Improvements in transportation helped the farming businesses, too. Roads were paved, which made it easier to transport the farmers' goods to the East Coast. The invention of steamboat helped to deliver goods quickly down to the South by way of the Mississippi River. The building of canals allowed farmers in southern Ohio to transport their crops up to Lake Erie, where large ships then took them to the East Coast. Another improvement was the construction of the railroads throughout Ohio. Trains became a quick and cheap way to move products to every state in the Union.

Agriculture remained a very good source of money in Ohio until the late 1800s. By then, other states in the West had been admitted to the Union, and Ohio farmers had trouble competing with the western states' low prices. Many Ohioans sold their farms and moved to the cities to find other types of work.

As Ohioans were getting used to living in their new state, the United States government faced the possibility of war over the issue of slavery. One of the conditions under which Ohio became a state was that the owning of slaves would be illegal. Because Ohio was a "free" state that did not allow slavery, many runaway slaves fought their way to the shores of the Ohio River. A very strong anti-slavery movement developed in Ohio just before the Civil War. Many Ohioans were actively involved in what was called the Underground Railroad. Although not really involved with trains, the Underground Railroad helped runaway slaves to

These Union soldiers served in the 125th Ohio Infantry during the Civil War.

freedom. This program was carried out through many free states in the nation. Groups of people who disagreed with slavery hid runaway slaves in their homes. They fed them, offered them clothes, and tended to their wounds and illnesses before helping them travel to free lands.

The Twentieth Century and Beyond

Ohio cities began to grow in the beginning of the twentieth century. Tall skyscrapers and other modern office buildings were built. Cleveland, in the 1920s, was the fifth-largest city in the United States.

However, in the early 1930s, Ohio suffered from the effects of the Great Depression, a time when jobs were very hard to find and many people went without food and other

Factories in the cities—such as this cash register factory in Dayton—employed men, women, and children.

necessities. Ohio had been one of the leading industrial states at that time. The Depression forced factories to close, and great numbers of Ohioans became unemployed. Many Ohioans moved back to their family farms so they could at least find food. But others had no choice but to try to stay alive in the cities. Even farmers suffered, as Ohio was experiencing a severe drought and crops were dying. Many Ohioans moved to other states in search of jobs. It was a tough time for the whole country.

The United States government developed some programs that helped the unemployed. They gave them jobs building roads, logging forests, and other activities that helped to improve the country. Several years later, another major event brought prosperity to Ohio. World War II was being fought in Europe, and the soldiers needed food and other supplies. Although many young Ohio farmers and the sons of farmers were sent to this war, immigrant workers from Mexico worked on the Ohio farms and in the food-processing factories. Women and African

During the Great Depression, these unemployed men were served soup and bread by relief workers in Cleveland.

Americans, who usually had a hard time finding work, were also given jobs. Another major business that benefited from the war was the Ohio airplane industry, which supplied the government with planes.

After the war, new businesses found Ohio attractive and more people poured into the state. In the 1960s, Ohio was one of the most populated states. Cities were getting so crowded, though, that builders began buying the land around the cities and creating suburbs. At this same time, interstate highways were built, providing quicker routes from one major city to another.

Although Ohio's large industries improved the economy, they also polluted the environment. Ohioans were told that Lake Erie was dying due to toxic wastes that were being dumped into the water. Then in 1969, when the Cuyahoga River was so full of chemical waste that it actually caught on fire, Ohioans realized they had many serious environment issues that they must face. Since then, Ohioans have voted to help pay for projects that improve the natural environment. Many Ohioans also work to make sure that everyone is aware of the problems of pollution and how to fix them.

The growth of the manufacturing industry helped Ohio's economy, but in many ways, it also hurt the state's environment.

In 2003, Ohioans celebrated as their state reached its two-hundredth anniversary of statehood. One way to celebrate this event was accomplished by artist Scott Hagan, who painted the state's bicentennial logo on at least one barn in each Ohio county to honor the agricultural roots of Ohio's history. There were also numerous fairs and parades and an old-fashioned wagon train trip across the state. The Ohio government paid for new ceremonial bells that were given to each of Ohio's eighty-eight counties.

Today, the people of Ohio are working hard to provide a safe, healthy, and prosperous environment to call their home. Cleaning up the environment, improving the schools, providing new jobs and health benefits, and renewing the downtown areas of Ohio's oldest cities are just some of the important issues that they are focusing on. They know and appreciate that Ohio is a great place to live, and they want to keep it that way. With a long and well-preserved history, Ohioans know how to face any challenge and come out ahead.

Ohio cities, such as Cincinnati, continue to draw a wide range of businesses and settlers.

Important Dates

13,000-7,000 BCE Paleo-Indians live in what would later become Ohio.

800 BC-100 CE The Adena culture thrives and builds huge mounds.

100-400 The Hopewell people establish trade routes with groups as far away as the East Coast, the Gulf Coast, and Canada.

1000-1600 The Fort Ancient people establish villages in the southern Ohio area and the Whittlesey Focus group gather in the north.

1641-1700 The Iroquois force out all other Native Americans from the Ohio area and claim the land as their hunting grounds.

1700-1761 The French explore the region and establish trading posts in the Ohio Country.

La Salle, a French explorer

1763-1776 For a short period of time, the British control the land that will become Ohio.

1776 The United States wins the Revolutionary War and claim British lands.

1803 Ohio becomes a state.

1832 The Ohio and Erie Canal is completed.

1869 The Cincinnati Red Stockings (later called the Cincinnati Reds) become the first professional baseball team.

1890 The first indoor shopping mall is built in Cleveland.

1955 The Ohio Turnpike is opened.

1962 Lt. Col. John Glenn, born in Cambridge, Ohio, becomes the first American to orbit the earth.

1969 Neil Armstrong, born in Wapakoneta, Ohio, becomes first man to walk on the moon.

1970 The first Monday Night Football game is played in Cleveland between the Cleveland Browns and the New York Jets.

1980s Once called the Rubber Capital of the World, Akron reduces the number of rubber products it manufactures.

1993 Ohio novelist Toni Morrison receives the Nobel Prize for literature for her life's work.

2003 Ohioans celebrate the bicentennial of their state.

John Glenn

3 The People

Ohio's population has been steadily growing over the years. In 1800, only a little more than 45,000 people lived in the state. In 1840, the population finally topped one million. Then it hit almost seven million in 1940. Now, Ohioans number more than eleven million and have the seventh-largest population in all of the fifty states. So you might ask, where did all these people come from? The answer is that they came from a lot of different places.

Native Americans

Native Americans were the first people to populate the area of present-day Ohio. Remains of ancient cultures have provided scientists with enough information for them to guess that people lived in this area at least 13,000 years ago. Ohio provided fertile lands full of animals and wild plants for the original people to find food and shelter for their families. Most of these early people were constantly moving to find food, so they lived in tents that could be easily folded and

These young Ohioans pose for a picture on the Turtle Creek Valley Railway.

43

Some Native American groups in Ohio continue to practice the traditions of their ancestors. At museums, festivals, and other cultural events, many also share their history and culture with non-Native people.

carted to new hunting grounds. These people survived on their skills as hunters.

Most of Native Americas who lived in the Ohio area around the seventeenth and eighteenth centuries were farmers. The largest groups included the Shawnee, Mingo, Delaware, the Iroquois, and the Miami. Many of these people lived in permanent houses that were made of poles cut from young trees and from tree bark, which they used to keep out the wind and rain. While on hunting expeditions, a teepee, or tent, was used to protect them from bad weather. Most Native American villages were usually located near a river or a stream, so they had a fresh supply of water. Before these groups began trading furs with Europeans, they made everything that they needed for everyday use. They made all their tools, canoes, and clothing.

As European settlers moved into the Ohio land, Native Americans found it difficult to maintain their lifestyle. Although they attempted to unite themselves in an effort to protect their homes, they were unsuccessful. Some Native people were moved to reservation land in Ohio. But by the late 1800s, all reservations in Ohio were closed, and most Native Americans were forced to move to reservations in other states.

Today there are less than 25,000 Native Americans living in Ohio. For the most part, they live just as other Ohioans live. They attend school, find jobs, and enjoy the lifestyle that their state offers. However, many still practice their traditions and honor their culture. Annual festivals and other gatherings give Ohio's Native Americans opportunities to celebrate their history and heritage.

The Europeans

The French were the first Europeans to live in Ohio. Most of them were either fur-trappers, fur traders, or missionaries who came to convert the Native American people to Christian religions. After the French and Indian War, however, most French people lost their foothold in Ohio Country and retreated north to Canada.

The British defeated the French in that war and then claimed the land that would become Ohio. Even though England later lost the right to this land after the

Revolutionary War, many of the British soldiers fell in love with the area and eventually settled down there. Indeed, most of the people who moved to this area after the war were from Great Britain. Some of these people were English. Other new settlers were from Ireland. Most of them had been farmers in Europe and continued to farm the Ohio land. Others found jobs in Ohio's factories.

Although everyone faced hardships, generally speaking, the Irish found it more difficult than the English. Prejudice against the Irish, mostly because of their Catholic religious practices, often made it very challenging for Irish immigrants to find good jobs. Many Irish men were forced to take the most physically demanding and poorly paid jobs that were available, such as digging Ohio's canals and laying the tracks for the railroads. Despite their hardships, the Irish immigrants helped to improve Ohio's economy due to their hard labor.

Did you know that Ohio is often called the Mother of U.S. Presidents? That is because seven presidents were born in Ohio. They are Ulysses S. Grant from Point Pleasant; Rutherford B. Hayes from Delaware; James A. Garfield from Orange; Benjamin Harrison, born in North Bend; William McKinley from Niles; William H. Taft, born in Cincinnati; and Warren G. Harding, who was born in Corsica, which is now called Blooming Grove.

Ohio's Holmes County, located between Columbus and Cleveland, is the home of the largest Amish community in the world. The Amish people originally immigrated to the

United States from Switzerland and Germany during the eighteenthcentury. They came here seeking religious freedom. Their beliefs differed from other Christian religions in Europe, and they hoped they would find a better life in America.

Today, the Amish people live separate from other communities. Most do not believe in using modern conveniences such as electricity and automobiles. They practice their traditional ways of life and mostly live off of the land. Many farming communities are run by the Amish.

Amish girls pause beside their family's buggy during a festival in Apple Creek.

Famous Ohioans

Neil Armstrong: Astronaut

Born in Wapakoneta, in 1930, Armstrong was a pilot for the U.S. Navy and a professor of Aerospace Engineering. In 1969, he was aboard the Apollo 11 spacecraft, which was headed for the moon. On July 20, Armstrong became the first person to step onto the moon.

Rita Dove: Author

Rita Dove was born in Akron, and was named the United States Poet Laureate in 1993. This made her the youngest person and the first African American to be given this honor. To be named the country's Poet Laureate is the highest honor that an American poet can receive. Before beginning her college education at Miami University in Oxford, Ohio, Rita was invited to the White House when she was only eighteen years old. This was because she was one of the best one hundred students to graduate from high school that year.

Cy Young: Athlete

Young was an outstanding baseball pitcher for a professional team called the Cleveland Spiders. His teammates called him "cyclone" because of the fast speed and spin of his pitch. Because of his great lifetime performance, an award was named in his honor. Each year the best pitcher from the American and the National Leagues are given a Cy Young Award.

Maya Lin: Architect

Maya Ying Lin was born in 1959 in Athens. She attended Yale University where she studied architecture. While she was a student, she entered a national design competition for a memorial that was to be built in honor of Vietnam veterans. She was only twenty-one years old when she found out that her design had won. The memorial was completed in 1982 in Washington, D.C.

Ulysses S. Grant: General and President of the United States

Born in Point Pleasant, Grant was the eighteenth president of the United States. Grant was a very good military leader for the Union during the Civil War. He was elected president of the United States in 1868. Grant's body is buried in New York City in the largest mausoleum— tomb—in North America.

Jesse Owens: Athlete

Jesse Owens grew up in Cleveland and attended Fairview Junior High, Cleveland East Technical High School, and Ohio State University. He was once called the fastest man on earth. Owens won four Olympic Gold Medals in 1936 in track and field. He won his gold medals in the long jump, the 100-meter and the 200-meter dash, and the 100-meter relay race. As a successful African American, Owens proved to many that African Americans could achieve great things.

By 1850, almost half of Ohio's immigrant population came from Germany. Most Germans settled around Ohio's major cities where they found jobs. Some were skilled craftsmen who helped create some of Ohio's major buildings. In 1900, the number of German immigrants was almost four times more than any other immigrant group. Although the number of German immigrants has decreased today, some cities still have large German populations. In Cincinnati, for example, almost half of the city's population is descended from German immigrants.

As industries grew in Ohio, people from other parts of Europe were also attracted to the state. By the 1920s, people from Italy, Poland, Hungary, and Russia were arriving in large numbers. So many people were moving to Ohio that in the early 1900s, almost three-fourths of Cleveland's citizens stated they were born in a country other than the United States or they were first generation United States citizens. This meant that even though they were born in the United States, their parents were immigrants from other countries.

The highest rate of immigration occurred in 1910. Then the number of immigrants began to decrease. However, about thirty years ago, immigration to Ohio once again began to rise. The federal government recently stated that Ohio appears to be one of the most popular choices of all immigrants who come to the United States.

African Americans

Before becoming a state, only a few hundred African Americans lived in Ohio. After the Civil War, however, more than 36,000

A brother and sister pose for a picture in Sandusky. Some African-American Ohioans trace their roots back to slaves who came to the area in the 1800s, while others moved to the region over the last few decades.

made Ohio their home. However, despite the fact that Ohio had been declared a slave-free state, African Americans had to deal with a lot of discrimination. Laws were passed against them, such as the one that denied them the right to vote. And in parts of southern Ohio, even though it was against the law, some white people owned slaves. Whenever authorities came around to check their farms, these farmers took their slaves to Kentucky to hide them.

Many African Americans moved to Ohio's cities in hopes of finding work. But life in the city was not always easy. Not only were good jobs hard to find, but some black people lived in constant fear of their former white slave-owners coming into town to take them back south.

But it was not just Southern slave-owners that caused African Americans trouble. In 1829, Irish Americans in Cincinnati became very angry because they thought that African Americans were taking jobs away from them. Riots broke out in the city. Many homes and businesses were destroyed and many people were killed or injured.

Despite these difficulties, many African Americans have prospered and become a valuable part of their communities. African Americans have not only prevailed, they have succeeded in business, education, the arts, sports, and government. Today over one million African Americans live in the state, making up the largest minority group in Ohio.

Diversity

Hispanics and Asians make up the next largest minorities in Ohio. Many Hispanics have come to Ohio not from Mexico or other Latino countries, but from other American cities, such as Chicago

Many people from around the country and around the world move to Ohio for better job opportunities and better schools and communities for their families.

and New York. Hispanics and Asians are the fastest growing minority groups in the United States as well as in Ohio. In a recent publication for Asian students, Ohio State University was named one of the top colleges in the United States for Asian students to attend.

The number of Hispanics in Ohio grew by more than 50 percent over the last few decades. They are now 1.9 percent of the state's population. The Asian population increased almost as much, and there are now 132,663 people of Asian descent living in Ohio.

Looking Toward the Future

"Ohio is among the nation's most multicultural states with an extremely diverse population," wrote a member of the Ohio Bicentennial Committee. To celebrate Ohio's many different cultures, the second Sunday of the Ohio State Fair has been declared Multicultural Day.

"Ohio is proud of the cultural diversity that enriches our state and the lives of our citizens," wrote Governor Bob Taft. The governor was encouraging the celebration of Ohio's many different cultures at the State Fair. In 2003, the fair celebrated Hispanic/Latino and Asian cultures. In 2004, the focus was on European and African/Middle Eastern cultures. "We come together to form a wonderful cultural mosaic," Governor Taft wrote, referring to all the different people and their diverse backgrounds that make up the population of Ohio.

Ohio has always been a good place to live. People from all over the world have come to live in this state. The land is fertile, the people are friendly, and the state is working hard to make sure that the young people of Ohio have a good future.

A good education is a big part of making sure that young Ohioans have a successful future. And in 2005, Ohio students proved they were doing their part to make this come true. They did better than the national average in reading and math tests as well as in other test scores. This means that

Ohio students are studying hard and their teachers are working hard to help Ohio's younger population to gain the skills that they will need later in life. The future looks very bright not just for the state's students, but for all Ohioans.

This family from Sugarcreek stops to enjoy a beautiful Ohio sunset.

Calendar of Events

Hinckley Township Buzzard Day Celebration

If you visit Hinckley in March you can watch as hundreds of buzzards come back to roost. These large birds—and their ancestors—have been coming back to Hinckley every year for at least two hundred years.

Cleveland International Film Festival

In March, Cleveland plays host to a large film festival that has been held every year for nearly thirty years. Thousands of people travel to Cleveland to view movies that premiere at this festival and actors, directors, and fans from around the world often attend.

Shelby's Radio Controlled 1/4-Scale Air Fair

In June people from all over the United States and Canada come to Shelby's Airport to see 1/4-scale model airplanes and the people who fly them. This fair is one of the most popular radio-controlled airplane rallies in the country.

Troy Strawberry Festival

Strawberries are an important crop in Ohio, and many towns and cities throughout the state have their own festivals to honor this fruit. But residents of Troy consider their city the Strawberry Capital of Ohio. Troy's Strawberry festival draws more than 200,000 people who take part in the parade, races, exhibits, arts and crafts, and contests the celebration offers.

Annual Great Mohican Indian Powwow

In July and September many gather at the Mohican Reservation Festival Grounds to celebrate and learn about Native American heritage. This festival in Loudonville includes traditional crafts, dancing, singing, storytelling, and fun for the whole family.

A parade

All-American Soapbox Derby

In July Akron is home to the All-American Soapbox Derby Championships where all the winners of local races meet to compete for this big annual event. Many soapbox racing enthusiasts gather at Derby Downs. Whether you competed in local competitions, or even if you have never raced at all, this is a fun summer event.

Twins Day Festival

Every August, since 1976, Twinsburg has celebrated twins with the Twins Day Festival. On the first Twins Day Festival, thirty-seven different sets of twins showed up. In 2005, more than 2000 sets of twins came to enjoy the food, the parade, and the talent show. Even the television show *Discovery* showed up to film this special event for twins of all ages.

Prairie Peddler Festival

This celebration is usually held on a few weekends in late September and early October. The festival gives visitors a feel of what life was like when Ohio first became a state. Held in Butler, this family-friendly gathering has a lot to offer. When you attend you can take part in craft activities and enjoy the entertainment, food, and exhibits.

Tall Stacks Festival

In October, this Cincinnati festival celebrates the beautiful Ohio River and the city's river history. Activities include river boat tours, boat races, and a lot of food and entertainment. There are also historical exhibits along the shoreline and fireworks at night.

A Twins Days festival in Twinsburg

57

4 How It Works

Ohio's constitution was first created in 1802, one year before Ohio was admitted to the Union. In this constitution, it was written that the state government should be divided into three separate branches. These are the executive branch, which administers laws, the legislative branch, which makes laws, and the judicial branch, which enforces and interprets laws.

The General Assembly met for the first time on March 1, 1803, in Chillicothe, Ohio's first capital. In 1810, Zanesville was made the capital, but for only two years. Then in 1816, Columbus was chosen as Ohio's state capital.

There are also local governments in each of the eighty-eight counties in Ohio, as well as in each town and city. Most counties are governed by an elected board of commissioners. Many of Ohio's cities elect a mayor, who serves with a council to enforce the laws and manage the budget.

Much of the money that the mayors use to run their cities comes from taxes. Where do these taxes come from? Well, when your parents receive paychecks from their jobs, state taxes are

Though Ohio became a state in 1803, Columbus did not become its official capital until 1816.

Branches of Government

Executive This branch is headed by a governor. The governor is responsible for the state budget, for signing bills that are passed in the General Assembly, and for appointing the directors of several state departments and agencies.

Legislative This branch is made up of the house of representatives and the senate, which are called the General Assembly. When the first meeting of the General Assembly was held in Chillicothe on March 1, 1803, there were only thirty representatives in the house and fourteen members in the senate. In 1967, voters approved an amendment to the state constitution, which increased those numbers. Now Ohio has ninety-nine members in the house and thirty-three members in the senate. The main role of these men and women is to debate bills that have been proposed. If the General Assembly votes in favor of a bill, the governor may sign it into law.

Judicial This branch is made up of the Ohio Supreme Court; and many lower courts, including courts of appeals, courts of common pleas, county courts, municipal courts, and the court of claims. The main job of the State Supreme Court judges is to make the final decisions in cases that the lower district courts could not resolve. State Supreme Court judges also hear all cases in which the death sentence has been imposed on criminals.

taken out of their wages. These are called income taxes. Also, whenever you buy certain products from stores, if you look at the receipt that you are given, you will notice that a sales tax has been added. This is one way that your town receives money to help pay for things like removing snow from your neighborhood streets in the winter and for paying lifeguards who watch over you at your city swimming pool in the summer. Taxes also pay for schools, government buildings, and government services for state residents.

How a Law Is Created

Members of the house and senate may either create new laws or change old ones. A law begins as a bill, which might be proposed by a state representative, a state senator, or an Ohio citizen. The proposal is then written up in legal language, recorded, and debated by a special committee. During this time, the bill might also be presented to voters so that the committee members can find out what the voters think about the bill. After all discussions are completed, the bill is debated in the house and senate. If the bill begins in the house, then representatives vote on the bill first. If the bill begins in the Senate, then the senators vote first.

If both the house and the senate pass the bill, it is sent to the governor for his or her signature. If the governor signs the bill, it becomes a law. However, there might be many more steps that a bill has to go through before it becomes a law. What if the house passes the bill but the senate does not? In this case there would be many more debates and maybe some changes would be made to the bill. Then the senate might request another vote. Sometimes when a bill is sent to a special committee, the members of that committee conclude that the bill would not make a good law. The bill would then not be sent to either the house or the senate for debate and a vote. Then the bill is said to have "died in committee."

Also, what happens if the House and the Senate pass the

The Ohio statehouse is where the state legislature meets. This historic landmark was built from 1839 to 1861 using materials that included Columbus limestone.

bill, but the governor vetoes it, or rejects it? In this case, the bill might be sent back to the General Assembly. The House and Senate would vote on the bill again. If they can get three-fifths of the representatives and three-fifths of the senators to vote in favor of the bill, the General Assembly can override the governor's veto. This means that the bill would become law even though the governor was against it.

So if there is an issue you feel strongly about, or a law you want to discuss, think about contacting your state legislators. They are there to serve you and the state. Together you can make a difference in your state.

If you would like to contact Ohio's state legislators go this Web site:
http://www.legislature.state.oh.us
You will need to know your zip code or district number to find your senator or representative. If you need help, ask a parent, teacher, or librarian.

5 Making a Living

Two main industries have played a very important role in Ohio's economic history—agriculture and manufacturing. Since the first permanent settlers in the Ohio region planted and cultivated seeds, agriculture has helped the people of Ohio make a living. Farm products are used throughout Ohio, and sold to other states as well. Although early farmers used tools such as hoes, rakes, and horse-drawn plows, as time went by, more modern farmers needed machinery and fuel. Their need for machines stimulated the growth of factories. The need for fuel encouraged the mining of coal. So agriculture was one big business that helped to create other businesses, expanding Ohio's economy.

Agriculture has gone through good and bad times over the years that Ohio has been a state. The Great Depression hit Ohio farmers at the same time as a very long drought. World Wars, on the other hand, increased the demand for food, and Ohio farmers benefited from this need. In the second half of the twentieth century, however, Ohioans saw

Agriculture has been—and continues to be—an important part of Ohio's economy.

the decline in the number of farms in their state. The cost of food had dropped while the cost of living rose. This meant that farmers were getting lower prices for their food at the same time that they had to pay higher prices for clothing, electricity, and machinery. This made many Ohioans turn to other ways of making a living. Many people sold their farms and moved to the cities.

Today, Ohio still has about 80,000 farms, which cover about half of all the land that makes up the state. The major crops that are grown on these farms include soybeans, corn, hay, oats, and wheat. Most of these grains are fed to cattle, another important product of agriculture. Ohio's cattle provide milk and beef. Ohio also is a major producer of hogs

Though it is hard work and can be very expensive to run a farm, many families continue to carry on the farming traditions established by Ohio settlers hundreds of years ago.

Ohioans who run small family farms often sell their fresh and delicious produce at local farm stands.

and ranks very high in the production of eggs.

Apples are another important state product. Legend says that around the same time that Ohio first became a state, Johnny Appleseed—who was actually a nurseryman named John Chapman—was traveling all over Ohio, planting apple orchards. Although some of those trees are now two hundred years old, they still bear fruit. But apples are not the only fruit that farmers produce today. Grapes and strawberries are also important crops. Vegetables such as cucumbers and tomatoes are also big Ohio crops.

Recipe for Spicy Apple Cider

Johnny Appleseed promoted the tasty apple by planting apple trees throughout Ohio's landscape. On a cold winter's night or even on a cool summer day, nothing tastes better than sipping a cup of hot spicy apple cider. Ask an adult to help you to prepare this easy but delicious drink.

Ingredients:
1 gallon apple cider or apple juice)
10 whole cloves
3 cinnamon sticks
1 tablespoon sugar
1 fresh lemon

Pour the apple cider into a large pot and have an adult help you set it on the stove. Add the whole cloves and the cinnamon sticks. Sprinkle the sugar into the pot and stir. Cut the fresh lemon and squeeze the juice into the pot.

Turn the burner on a low heat and let the apple cider cook for 1 hour. Stir the mixture every 15 minutes to make sure that nothing is sticking to the bottom of the pot. After 1 hour, turn off the burner and let it the cider cool down for a few minutes.

Ask an adult to pour the cider through a strainer into a large container. The strainer will catch all the lemon seeds, cloves, and what is left of the cinnamon sticks. After you have enjoyed your hot cup of spicy apple cider, you can store the rest of the cider in the refrigerator. When you want another cup, you can easily heat it up again either on the stove or in a microwave.

Manufacturing

Agriculture may be the oldest way people in Ohio make money, but manufacturing has also played a major role in the state economy. The state's manufacturing industry includes all products made in Ohio, such as cars, trucks, and parts for airplanes. Some Ohioans work in factories that produce steel and tools. Other people make chemicals that are used in paints and soaps. Did you know that Cincinnati has the largest soap factory in the United States?

Of course, there are also many food-processing plants in Ohio to handle the products that are grown on Ohio's farms. Types of food-processing plants include those that pack meat, preserve and can fruits, or process dairy products.

There are many different kinds of factories in Ohio. The city of Napoleon, for example, is home to the world's largest soup factory. And Wellston claims to be the world's leading producer of frozen pizzas. Other major products that are made in Ohio include computer parts, rubber, electrical equipment, clay, glass, and paper and plastic products.

Many Ohioans lost their jobs in manufacturing during the 1970s and 1980s. Businesses left the state because they found they could make more money in other states or in other countries. Despite the decrease in the number of factories, many Ohioans still work in manufacturing.

Factories and research centers employ hundreds of thousands of Ohioans.

Products & Resources

Corn

Corn is one of the largest crops grown in Ohio, and it grows all over the state. Corn is Ohio's second most-valuable crop, after soybeans. Ohio ranks sixth among all the states in how much corn they grow. In 2004, that total was well over 400 million bushels. Most of this corn is not eaten by people, though. More than half of it goes to feeding livestock like cows. Another portion is used in making things like plastic and ethanol, which is a type of fuel. Corn is also made into cereal and cooking oil, as well as into glue and ink.

Soybeans

Although most of the soybeans grown in Ohio are fed to cattle, soybeans are also used to make a nondairy substitute for milk. Soybeans are also used in nonfood items such as hand cleaners, chemical cleaners that remove graffiti spray paint, and lubricants that oil machines so they work more smoothly.

Coal

This is Ohio's most important mined resource. All of Ohio's coal mines are located in the eastern part of the state. Despite the fact that miners have been digging for coal for a long time, scientists believe there are still over 20 billion tons of coal still buried underground.

Salt

Every time a heavy snow falls on Ohio's roads, trucks hurry out and spread salt on the pavement to make the snow melt. Have you ever wondered where all that salt comes from? About 2,000 feet underground in eastern Ohio, there are very large deposits of salt, which scientists predict will last for about another thousand years. Ohio is one of the nation's largest producers of rock salt, and the state mines about 4 million tons of it each year.

Cars and Trucks

Ohio is the second-largest producer of vehicles in the United States. In 2004, one-fourth of all manufacturing jobs in Ohio were in the automobile industry. The biggest automobile manufacturing companies in Ohio include General Motors, Ford, Honda, and Chrysler. Ohioans, living in cities like Toledo and Dayton, made over 800,000 Accords, Cavaliers, Liberties, and Trailblazers and almost one million small trucks.

Strawberries

Ohio farmers rank ninth in the United States for growing strawberries. Over 800 acres of farmland are devoted just to strawberries. This crop produced over $5 million for farmers in 2004. Strawberries are sometimes hard to grow. But researchers at Ohio's universities are trying to come up with new types of strawberries that will grow better in Ohio and may boost the state's production, making it one of the more important states to grow this delicious fruit.

Service

Most people who have jobs in Ohio work for the service industry. People in this industry provide some sort of service for others. Examples of service industry jobs include those in health-care facilities, hotels, stores, gas stations, grocery stores, and schools.

Tourism is a major part of the state's service industry. Every year, millions of people visit or travel through Ohio. Visitors may want to relax on Ohio's lakeshore, hike through its parks, or visit the state's many historic sites or museums. Others enjoy the different festivals and other events in Ohio's cities and towns. Whatever their reason, these people spend money in the state. That money provides a profit for these service businesses and for the

Transportation plays an major role in Ohio's economy. The state's waterways are especially important for transporting the goods that are mined or made in the Buckeye State.

state. Besides bringing money into the state, the tourism industry also provides a lot of service jobs for Ohioans. Tour guides, museum curators, hotel clerks, waiters, waitresses, and store clerks all have service jobs that depend on this industry.

The Future

The kind of jobs that Ohioans might have in the future could be a lot different from those of the past. In his 2000 State of the State speech, Governor Bob Taft pointed out that the future of Ohio's economy may be based on technology. "Cell phones, pagers, laptops, the Internet and digital technology have revolutionized the way we listen, learn and live. Technology is changing the world as we know it." Governor Taft believed that Ohio schools need to train students so they understand the modern technologies and to encourage students to go on to college to complete their education.

As in many other states, Ohioans are trying to figure out how to protect their environment and, at the same time, encourage growth. Having more businesses might mean more jobs and therefore more money, but does it also mean more pollution to the natural environment? This is one of the questions that Ohioans must answer. And jobs in technology may prove to be

The Rock and Roll Hall of Fame and Museum in Cleveland has attracted more than five million visitors since it opened in 1995.

one of many solutions that help Ohioans to have comfortable lives and still preserve the beauty of their state.

As time goes by, everything changes. This is true for Ohio as it is true for every other state in the country and every nation in the world. Jobs, for instance, that Ohioans could once trust on always being available are beginning to disappear. Although work in manufacturing is still important in Ohio, Ohio's leaders are making sure that they have an eye on the future. They know that jobs in high technology are becoming more essential. This means that they need to bring high technology businesses into the state and to provide high technology education in Ohio's schools.

Living in Ohio today means living in a very exciting world. Everyone in Ohio has a role to play in creating these changes and helping to lead Ohio through the twenty-first century.

Ohio has more than seventy state parks. Many residents and visitors especially enjoy the beachfront parks, such as Edgewater Park, on the shore of Lake Erie.

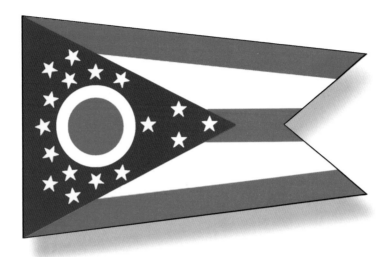

Instead of being rectangular in shape, the flag looks more like a pennant with a swallowtail design. On the left of the flag is a large, blue triangle with seventeen white stars. Thirteen of those white stars represent the thirteen original colonies. The other four white stars are for the states that joined the Union later, with Ohio being the seventeenth state to do so. The white "O" stands for "Ohio." The red and white stripes represent the roads and waterways of the state.

The seal is made up of three circles. The inner circle has a picture that includes a rising sun with thirteen rays, representing the thirteen original colonies. The sun is rising over Mount Logan. In the middle ground is the Scioto River. There is also a field and a sheaf of wheat, which stand for agriculture and bounty. The sheaf of seventeen arrows refers to Ohio being the seventeenth state to join the Union.

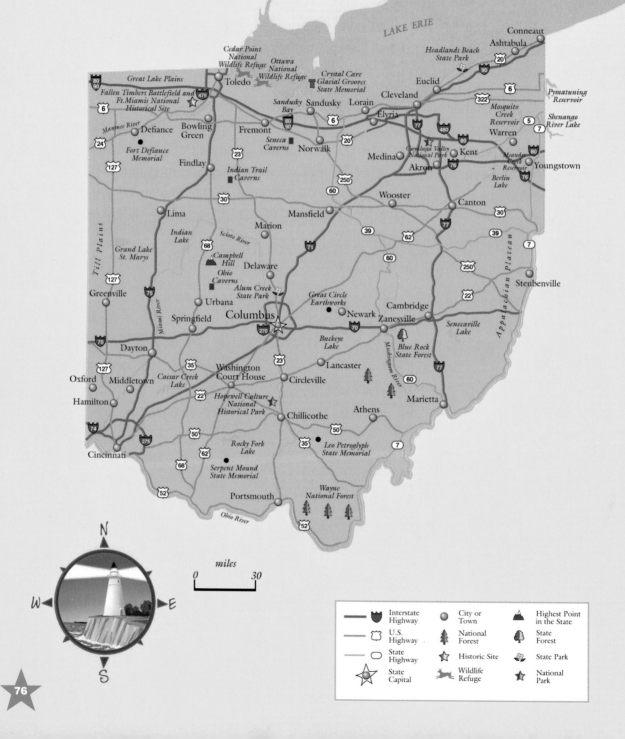

OHIO

LAKE ERIE

Conneaut
Ashtabula
Great Lake Plains
Cedar Point National Wildlife Refuge
Ottawa National Wildlife Refuge
Headlands Beach State Park
80 90
Toledo
Crystal Cave Glacial Grooves State Memorial
Euclid
Cleveland
20
90
6
322
Pymatuning Reservoir
Fallen Timbers Battlefield and Ft.Miamis National Historical Site
475
6
Sandusky Bay
Sandusky
Lorain
Elyria
77
480
Mosquito Creek Reservoir
Shenango River Lake
Maumee River
Defiance
Bowling Green
Fremont
80 90
6
Cuyahoga Valley National Park
Warren
5
7
24
23
Seneca Caverns
Norwalk
20
Medina
Kent
80
Meander Creek Reservoir
Youngstown
127
Findlay
250
Akron
76
Berlin Lake
76
Fort Defiance Memorial
Indian Trail Caverns
60
Wooster
Canton
Till Plains
Lima
30
Mansfield
39
62
30
39
7
Indian Lake
Marion
71
60
250
Steubenville
Grand Lake St. Marys
68
Campbell Hill
Scioto River
60
22
Appalachian Plateau
127
Ohio Caverns
Delaware
Greenville
75
Alum Creek State Park
Great Circle Earthworks
Cambridge
Urbana
Columbus
Newark
Zanesville
Senecaville Lake
Miami River
Springfield
270
70
Buckeye Lake
Blue Rock State Forest
Dayton
70
23
Lancaster
Muskingum River
77
Oxford
35
Washington Court House
Circleville
60
Middletown
Caesar Creek Lake
22
Marietta
Hamilton
Hopewell Culture National Historical Park
Chillicothe
Athens
74
275
50
Rocky Fork Lake
35
50
Leo Petroglyph State Memorial
7
Cincinnati
62
68
Serpent Mound State Memorial
Portsmouth
Wayne National Forest
52
Ohio River
52

N
W E
S

miles
0   30

Legend

Interstate Highway	●	City or Town	▲	Highest Point in the State	
U.S. Highway	🌲	National Forest		State Forest	
State Highway	☆	Historic Site		State Park	
State Capital	🦌	Wildlife Refuge	✦	National Park	

76

Beautiful Ohio

Words by Ballard MacDonald
Music by Robert King

Long, long a - go   Some - one I know   Had a lit - tle red ca -

noe,   In it room for on - ly two.   Love found its start

Then in my heart,   And like a flow - er grew. _____

CHORUS
Drift - ing with the cur - rent down a moon - lit stream,   While a - bove the

Heav - ens in their glo - ry gleam,   And the stars on

high _____   Twin - kle in the sky, _____   Seem - ing in a

Par - a - dise of love de - vine,   Dream - ing of a pair of eyes that

looked in mine.   Beau - ti - ful O - hi - o, in dreams a - gain I

see   Vi - sions of what used to be.

More About Ohio

Books About the State

Jackson, Tom. *The Ohio River*. Milwaukee, WI: Gareth Stevens, 2004.

Knapp, Ron. *Ohio*. Berkeley Heights, NJ: yReportLinks.com Books, 2002.

Schonberg, Marcia. *Uniquely Ohio*. Chicago: Heinemann Library, 2003.

Web sites

History of Ohio

http://www.ohiomemory.org/

OhioKIDS—History for Kids

http://www.ohiokids.org/index.shtml

Information about Ohio's General Assembly

http://www.legislature.state.oh.us

About the Author

Joyce Hart was born in Mansfield, Ohio. Her grandparents were German immigrants who moved to Ohio. In the winter, Ms. Hart would sled down the long, snow-packed hill behind her grandparent's house. In the summer, she and her family spent the weekends at Lake Erie. A few years ago, Ms. Hart's daughter went back to Ohio to attend Oberlin College. Currently, Joyce Hart lives in Washington.

Index

Page numbers in **boldface** are illustrations.